Introduction

Hammurabi's code has been translated into many

languages since it's discovery.

Most scholars agree the following is an accurate translation. However, considering the span of time between writing the code and its discovery and translation, there always remains the question of absolute accuracy.

It is considered by many as the earliest known written criminal and civil code ever discovered. It is estimated it was written by the King of Babylon, Hammurabi, in approximately 1780 B.C.E.

Found in 1901; it was carved into a large stone monolith.

The identified system of punishment in this text foreshadows the 'an eye for an eye' concept.

Hammurabi wisely established the foundation for criminal and civil law. He understood the importance of trade and commerce and include regulations relating to those activities.

Hammurabi's code is considered the precursor of Jewish, Islamic and America justice. Many countries have drawn inspiration from his codes.

As I studied the Code I found that even today, King Hammurabi's code is taught in law schools and police academy's as one of the basis for American civil and criminal law.

Here are my findings in brief;

Eighteen hundred years before the birth ofChrist, the Babylonian King authored nearly 300 laws establishing canons of justice for Mesopotamia. His laws ranged from criminal to civil. From property rights and criminal behavior to slavery and divorce. The King also believed in harsh publishment for those who violated the code.

Without question violators received harsh punishment. This is where the eye-for-an-eye dictum is thought to originated in a written code. As an example, if a man broke another's leg (if they were considered equals) that man's leg would be broken. Incest meant being burned alive. In cases involving the God's or witchcraft, if the accused survived a deadly ordeal, he was exonerated. If he died, he was considered guilty.

Classes of people, especially men, were treated differently. The rich received a lesser punishment than a common man. And women had few rights, except the right to receive a harsh punishment, including death, for the same infraction a man would simply be fined.

Fair wages were also a concern of the King and he established minimum wages for various trades and professions. The higher the education and skill level, the higher wages.

Perhaps his most enduring code was that a person is considered innocent until proven guilty. That is the foundation for all American criminal law.

A century ago, Rev. Claude Johns offered his interpretation of the King's Code. Johns based his arguments in the findings of other 18th century researchers. Before reading Hammurabi's code, it is advisable to read Johns version. He was insightful and probably reasonably accurate. However, we can not entirely rely on his findings as the authority on the subject. Attempting to interpret the meaning of a document written thousands of years earlier, is always difficult and in some cases impossible. We can only make judgements on what is entirely clear in Hammurabi's writings.

The following is what Rev. Johns wrote a century ago. Since Johns was British, his spelling of certain words is different from that of American spelling.

The material for the study of Babylonian law is singularly extensive without being exhaustive. The so-called "contracts," including a great variety of deeds, conveyances, bonds, receipts, accounts and, most important of all, the actual legal decisions given by the judges in the law courts, exist in thousands. Historical inscriptions, royal charters and rescripts, despatches, private letters and the general literature afford welcome supplementary information. Even grammatical and lexicographical works, intended solely to facilitate the study of ancient literature, contain many extracts or short sentences bearing on law and custom. The so-called "Sumerian Family Laws" are thus preserved. The discovery of the now celebrated Code of Hammurabi (hereinafter simply termed the Code) has, however, made a more systematic study possible than could have resulted from the classification and interpretation of the other material. Some fragments of a later code exist and have been published; but there still remain many points upon which we have no evidence.

This material dates from the earliest times down to the commencement of our era. The evidence upon a particular point may be very full at one period and almost entirely lacking at another. The Code forms the backbone of the skeleton sketch which is here reconstructed. The fragments of it which have been recovered from Assur-bani-pal's library at Nineveh and later Babylonian copies show that it was studied, divided into chapters entitled *Ninu ilu sirum* from its opening words, and recopied for fifteen hundred years or more. The greater part of It remained in force, even through the Persian, Greek and Parthian conquests, which affected private life in Babylonia very little, and it survived to influence Syro-Roman and later Mahommedan law in Mesopotamia. The law and custom which preceded the Code we shall call "early," that of the New Babylonian empire (as well as the Persian, Greek, &c.) "late." The law in Assyria was derived from Babylonia but conserved early features long after they had disappeared elsewhere.

When the Semitic tribes settled in the cities of Babylonia, their tribal custom passed over into city law. The early history of the country is the story of a struggle for supremacy between the cities. A metropolis demanded tribute and military support from its subject cities but left their local cults and customs unaffected. The city rights and usages were respected by kings and conquerors alike.

As late as the accession of Assur-bani-pal and Samas-sum-yukin we find the Babylonians appealing to their city laws that groups of aliens to the number of twenty at a time were free to enter the city, that foreign women once married to Babylonian husbands could not be enslaved and that not even a dog that entered the city could be put to death untried.

The population of Babylonia was of many races from early times and intercommunication between the cities was incessant. Every city had a large number of resident aliens. This freedom of intercourse must have tended to assimilate custom. It was, however, reserved for the genius of Hammurabi to make Babylon his metropolis and weld together his vast empire by a uniform system of law.

Almost all trace of tribal custom has already disappeared from the law of the Code. It is state-law; - alike self-help, blood-feud, marriage by capture, are absent; though family solidarity, district responsibility, ordeal, the lex talionis, are primitive features that remain. The king is a benevolent autocrat, easily accessible to all his subjects, both able and willing to protect the weak against the highest-placed oppressor. The royal power, however, can only pardon when private resentment is appeased. The judges are strictly supervised and appeal is allowed. The whole land is covered with feudal holdings, masters of the levy, police, &c. There is a regular postal system. The *pax Babylonica* is so assured that private individuals do not hesitate to ride in their carriage from Babylon to the coast of the Mediterranean. The position of women is free and dignified.

The Code did not merely embody contemporary custom or conserve ancient law. It is true that centuries of law-abiding and litigious habitude had accumulated in the temple archives of each city vast stores of precedent in ancient deeds and the records of judicial decisions, and that intercourse had assimilated city custom. The universal habit of writing and perpetual recourse to written contract even more modified primitive custom and ancient precedent. Provided the parties could agree, the Code left them free to contract as a rule. Their deed of agreement was drawn up in the temple by a notary public, and confirmed by an oath "by god and the king." It was publicly sealed and witnessed by professional witnesses, as well as by collaterally interested parties. The manner in which it was thus executed may have been sufficient security that its stipulations were not impious or illegal. Custom or public opinion doubtless secured that the parties would not agree to wrong. In case of dispute the judges dealt first with the contract. They might not sustain it, but if the parties did not dispute it, they were free to observe it. The judges' decision might, however, be appealed against. Many contracts contain the proviso that in case of future dispute the parties would abide by "the decision of the king." The Code made known, in a vast number of cases, what that decision would be, and many cases of appeal to the king were sent back to the judges with orders to decide in accordance with it. The Code itself was carefully and logically arranged and the order of its sections was conditioned by their subject-matter. Nevertheless the order is not that of modern scientific treatises, and a somewhat different order from both is most convenient for our purpose.

The Code contemplates the whole population as falling into three classes, the amelu, the muskinu and the ardu. The amelu was a patrician, the man of family, whose birth, marriage and death were registered, of ancestral estates and full civil rights. He had aristocratic privileges and responsibilities, the right to exact retaliation for corporal injuries, and liability to heavier punishment for crimes and misdemeanours, higher fees and fines to pay. To this class belonged the king and court, the higher officials, the professions and craftsmen. The term became in time a mere courtesy title but originally carried with it standing. Already in the Code, when status is not concerned, it is used to denote "any one." There was no property qualification nor does the term appear to be racial. It is most difficult to characterize the muskinu exactly. The term came in time to mean "a beggar" and with that meaning has passed through Aramaic and Hebrew into many modern languages; but though the Code does not regard him as necessarily poor, he may have been landless. He was free, but had to accept monetary compensation for corporal injuries, paid smaller fees and fines, even paid less offerings to the gods. He inhabited a separate quarter of the city. There is no reason to regard him as specially connected with the court, as a royal pensioner, nor as forming the bulk of the population. The rarity of any reference to him in contemporary documents makes further specification conjectural. The ardu was a slave, his master's chattel, and formed a very numerous class. He could acquire property and even hold other slaves. His master clothed and fed him, paid his doctor's fees, but took all compensation paid for injury done to him. His master usually found him a slave-girl as wife (the children were then born slaves), often set him up in a house (with farm or business) and simply took an annual rent of him. Otherwise he might marry a freewoman (the children were then free), who might bring him a dower which his master could not touch, and at his death one-half of his property passed to his master as his heir. He could acquire his freedom by purchase from his master, or might be freed and dedicated to a temple, or even adopted, when he became an amelu and not a muskinu. Slaves were recruited by purchase abroad, from captives taken in war and by freemen degraded for debt or crime. A slave often ran away; if caught, the captor was bound to restore him to his master, and the Code fixes a reward of two shekels which the owner must pay the captor. It was about one-tenth of the average value. To detain, harbour, &c., a slave was punished by death. So was an attempt to get him to leave the city. A slave bore an identification mark, which could only be removed by a surgical operation and which later consisted of his owner's name tattooed or branded on the arm. On the great estates in Assyria and its subject provinces were many serfs, mostly of subject race, settled captives, or quondam slaves, tied to the soil they cultivated and sold with the estate but capable of possessing land and property of their own. There is little trace of serfs in Babylonia, unless the muskinu be really a serf.

The god of a city was originally owner of its land, which encircled it with an inner ring of irrigable arable land and an outer fringe of pasture, and the citizens were his tenants. The god and his viceregent, the king, had long ceased to disturb tenancy, and were content with fixed dues in naturalia, stock, money or service. One of the earliest monuments records the purchase by a king of a large estate for his son, paying a fair market price and adding a handsome honorarium to the many owners in costly garments, plate, and precious articles of furniture. The Code recognizes complete private ownership in land, but apparently extends the right to hold land to votaries, merchants (and resident aliens?). But all land was sold subject to its fixed charges. The king, however, could free land from these charges by charter, which was a frequent way of rewarding those who deserved well of the state. It is from these charters that we learn nearly all we know of the obligations that lay upon land. The state demanded men for the army and the corvee as well as dues in kind. A definite area was bound to find a bowman together with his linked pikeman (who bore the shield for both) and to furnish them with supplies for the campaign. This area was termed "a bow" as early as the 8th century B.C., but the usage was much earlier. Later, a horseman was due from certain areas. A man was only bound to serve so many (six?) times, but the land had to find a man annually. The service was usually discharged by slaves and serfs, but the amelu (and perhaps the muskenu) went to war. The "bows" were grouped in tens and hundreds. The corvee was less regular. The letters of Hammurabi often deal with claims to exemption. Religious officials and shepherds in charge of flocks were exempt. Special liabilities lay upon riparian owners to repair canals, bridges, quays, &c. The state claimed certain proportions of all crops, stock, &c. The king's messengers could commandeer any subject's property, giving a receipt. Further, every city had its own octroi duties, customs, ferry dues, highway and water rates. The king had long ceased to be, if he ever was, owner of the land. He had his own royal estates, his private property and dues from all his subjects. The higher officials had endowments and official residences. The Code regulates the feudal position of certain classes. They held an estate from the king consisting of house, garden, field, stock and a salary, on condition of personal service on the king's errand. They could not delegate the service on pain of death. When ordered abroad they could nominate a son, if capable, to hold the benefice and carry on the duty. If there was no son capable, the state put in a locum tenens, but granted one-third to the wife to maintain herself and children. The benefice was inalienable, could not be sold, pledged, exchanged, sublet, devised or diminished. Other land was held of the state for rent. Ancestral estate was strictly tied to the family. If a holder would sell, the family had the right of redemption and there seems to have been no time-limit to its exercise.

The temple occupied a most important position. It received from its estates, from tithes and other fixed dues, as well as from the sacrifices (a customary share) and other offerings of the faithful, vast amounts of all sorts of naturalia; besides money and permanent gifts. The larger temples had many officials and servants. Originally, perhaps, each town clustered round one temple, and each head of a family had a right to minister there and share its receipts. As the city grew, the right to so many days a year at one or other shrine (or its "gate") descended in certain families and became a species of property which could be pledged, rented or shared within the family, but not alienated. In spite of all these demands, however, the temples became great granaries and store-houses; as they also were the city archives. The temple held its responsibilities. If a citizen was captured by the enemy and could not ransom himself the temple of his city must do so. To the temple came the poor farmer to borrow seed corn or supplies for harvesters, &c.--advances which he repaid without interest. The king's power over the temple was not proprietary but administrative. He might borrow from it but repaid like other borrowers. The tithe seems to have been the composition for the rent due to the god for his land. It is not clear that all lands paid tithe, perhaps only such as once had a special connexion with the temple.

The Code deals with a class of persons devoted to the service of a god, as vestals or hierodules. The vestals were vowed to chastity, lived together in a great nunnery, were forbidden to open or enter a tavern, and together with other votaries had many privileges.

The Code recognizes many ways of disposing of property-- sale, lease, barter, gift, dedication, deposit, loan, pledge, all of which were matters of contract. Sale was the delivery of the purchase (in the case of real estate symbolized by a staff, a key, or deed of conveyance) in return for the purchase money, receipts being given for both. Credit, if given, was treated as a debt, and secured as a loan by the seller to be repaid by the buyer, fr which he gave a bond. The Code admits no claim unsubstantiated by documents or the oath of witnesses. A buyer had to convince himself of the seller's title. If he bought (or received on deposit) from a minor or a slave without power of attorney, he would be executed as a thief. If the goods were stolen and the rightful owner reclaimed them, he had to prove his purchase by producing the seller and the deed of sale or witnesses to it. Otherwise he would be adjudged a thief and die. If he proved his purchase, he had to give up the property but had his remedy against the seller or, if he had died, could reclaim five-fold from his estate. A man who bought a slave abroad, might find that he had been stolen or captured from Babylonia, and he had to restore him to his former owner without profit. If he bought property belonging to a feudal holding, or to a ward in chancery, he had to return it and forfeit what he gave for it as well. He could repudiate the purchase of a slave attacked by the bennu sickness within the month (later, a hundred days), and had a female slave three days on approval. A defect of title or undisclosed liability would invalidate the sale at any time.

Landowners frequently cultivated their land themselves but might employ a husbandman or let it. The husbandman was bound to carry out the proper cultivation, raise an average crop and leave the field in good tilth. In case the crop failed the Code fixed a statutory return. Land might be let at a fixed rent when the Code enacted that accidental loss fell on the tenant. If let on share-profit, the landlord and tenant shared the loss proportionately to their stipulated share of profit. If the tenant paid his rent and left the land in good tilth, the landlord could not interfere nor forbid subletting. Waste land was let to reclaim, the tenant being rent-free for three years and paying a stipulated rent in the fourth year. If the tenant neglected to reclaim the land the Code enacted that he must hand it over in good tilth and fixed a statutory rent. Gardens or plantations were let in the same ways and under the same conditions; but for date-groves four years' free tenure was allowed. The metayer system was in vogue, especially on temple lands. The landlord found land, labour, oxen for ploughing and working the watering-machines, carting, threshing or other implements, seed corn, rations for the workmen and fodder for the cattle. The tenant, or steward, usually had other land of his own. If he stole the seed, rations or fodder, the Code enacted that his fingers should be cut off. If he appropriated or sold the implements, impoverished or sublet the cattle, he was heavily fined and in default of payment might be condemned to be torn to pieces by the cattle on the field. Rent was as contracted.

Irrigation was indispensable. If the irrigator neglected to repair his dyke, or left his runnel open and caused a flood, he had to make good the damage done to his neighbours' crops, or be sold with his family to pay the cost. The theft of a watering-machine, water-bucket or other agricultural implement was heavily fined.

Houses were let usually for the year, but also for longer terms, rent being paid in advance, half-yearly. The contract generally specified that the house was in good repair, and the tenant was bound to keep it so. The woodwork, including doors and door frames, was removable, and the tenant might bring and take away his own. The Code enacted that if the landlord would re-enter before the term was up, he must remit a fair proportion of the rent. Land was leased for houses or other buildings to be built upon it, the tenant being rent-free for eight or ten years; after which the building came into the landlord's possession.

Despite the multitude of slaves, hired labour was often needed, especially at harvest. This was matter of contract, and the hirer, who usually paid in advance, might demand a guarantee to fulfil the engagement. Cattle were hired for ploughing, working the watering-machines, carting, threshing, etc. The Code fixed a statutory wage for sowers, ox-drivers, field-labourers, and hire for oxen, asses, &c.

There were many herds and flocks. The flocks were committed to a shepherd who gave receipt for them and took them out to pasture. The Code fixed him a wage. He was responsible for all care, must restore ox for ox, sheep for sheep, must breed them satisfactorily. Any dishonest use of the flock had to be repaid ten-fold, but loss by disease or wild beasts fell on the owner. The shepherd made good all loss due to his neglect. If he let the flock feed on a field of corn he had to pay damages four-fold; if he turned them into standing corn when they ought to have been folded he paid twelve-fold.

In commercial matters, payment in kind was still common, though the contracts usually stipulate for cash, naming the standard expected, that of Babylon, Larsa, Assyria, Carchemish, &c. The Code enacted, however, that a debtor must be allowed to pay in produce according to statutory scale. If a debtor had neither money nor crop, the creditor-must not refuse goods.

Debt was secured on the person of the debtor. Distraint on a debtor's corn was forbidden by the Code; not only must the creditor give it back, but his illegal action forfeited his claim altogether. An unwarranted seizure for debt was fined, as was the distraint of a working ox. The debtor being seized for debt could nominate as mancipium or hostage to work off the debt, his wife, a child, or slave. The creditor could only hold a wife or child three years as mancipium. If the mancipium died a natural death while in the creditor's possession no claim could lie against the latter; but if he was the cause of death by cruelty, he had to give son for son, or pay for a slave. He could sell a slave-hostage, unless she were a slave-girl who had borne her master children. She had to be redeemed by her owner.

he debtor could also pledge his property, and in contracts often pledged a field house or crop. The Code enacted, however, that the debtor should always take the crop himself and pay the creditor from it. If the crop failed, payment was deferred and no interest could be charged for that year. If the debtor did not cultivate the field himself he had to pay for the cultivation, but if the cultivation was already finished he must harvest it himself and pay his debt from the crop. If the cultivator did not get a crop this would not cancel his contract. Pledges were often made where the intrinsic value of the article was equivalent to the amount of the debt; but antichretic pledge was more common, where the profit of the pledge was a set-off against the interest of the debt. The whole property of the debtor might be pledged as security for the payment of the debt, without any of it coming into the enjoyment of the creditor. Personal guarantees were often given that the debtor would repay or the guarantor become liable himself.

Trade was very extensive. A common way of doing business was for a merchant to entrust goods or money to a travelling agent, who sought a market for his goods. The caravans travelled far beyond the limits of the empire. The Code insisted that the agent should inventory and give a receipt for all that he received. No claim could be made for anything not so entered. Even if the agent made no profit he was bound to return double what he had received, if he made poor profit he had to make up the deficiency; but he was not responsible for loss by robbery or extortion on his travels. On his return, the principal must give a receipt for what was handed over to him. Any false entry or claim on the agent's part was penalised three-fold, on the principal's part six-fold. In normal cases profits were divided according to contract, usually equally.

A considerable amount of forwarding was done by the caravans. The carrier gave a receipt for the consignment, took all responsibility and exacted a receipt on delivery. If he defaulted he paid five-fold. He was usually paid in advance. Deposit, especially warehousing of grain, was charged for at one-sixtieth. The warehouseman took all risks, paid double for all shortage, but no claim could be made unless be had given a properly witnessed receipt. Water traffic on the Euphrates and canals was early very considerable. Ships, whose tonnage was estimated at the amount of grain they could carry, were continually hired for the a transport of all kinds of goods. The Code fixes the price for building and insists on the builder's giving a year's guarantee of seaworthiness. It fixes the hire of ship and of crew. The captain was responsible for the freight and the ship; he had to replace all loss. Even if he refloated the ship he had to pay a fine of half its value for sinking it. In the case of collision the boat under way was responsible for damages to the boat at anchor. The Code also regulated the liquor traffic, fixing a fair price for beer and forbidding the connivance of the tavern-keeper (a female!) at disorderly conduct or treasonable assembly, under pain of death. She was to hale the offenders to the palace, which implied an efficient and accessible police system.

Payment through a banker or by written draft against deposit was frequent. Bonds to pay were treated as negotiable. Interest a was rarely charged on advances by the temple or wealthy land-owners for pressing needs, but this may have been part of the metayer system. The borrowers may have been tenants. Interest was charged at very high rates for overdue loans of this kind. Merchants (and even temples in some cases) made ordinary business loans, charging from 20 to 30%.

Marriage retained the form of purchase, but was essentially a contract to be man and wife together. The marriage of young people was usually arranged between the relatives, the bridegroom's father providing the bride-price, which with other presents the suitor ceremonially presented to the bride's father. This bride-price was usually handed over by her father to the bride on her marriage, and so came back into the bridegroom's possession, along with her dowry, which was her portion as a daughter. The bride-price varied much, according to the position of the parties, but was in excess of that paid for a slave. The Code enacted that if the father does not, after accepting a man's presents, give him his daughter, he, must return the presents doubled. Even if his decision was brought about by libel on the part of the suitor's friend this was done, and the Code enacted that the faithless friend should not marry the girl. If a suitor changed his mind, he forfeited the presents. The dowry might include real estate, but generally consisted of personal effects and household furniture. It remained the wife's for life, descending to her children, if any; otherwise returning to her family, when the husband could deduct the bride-price if it had not been given to her, or return it, if it had. The marriage ceremony included joining of hands and the utterance of some formula of acceptance on the part of the bridegroom, as "I am the son of nobles, silver and gold shall fill thy lap, thou shalt be my wife, I will be thy husband. Like the fruit of a garden I will give thee offspring." It must be performed by a freeman.

The marriage contract, without which the Code ruled that the woman was no wife, usually stated the consequences to which each party was liable for repudiating the other. These by no means necessarily agree with the Code. Many conditions might be inserted: as that the wife should act as maidservant to her mother-in-law, or to a first wife. The married couple formed a unit as to external responsibility, especially for debt. The man was responsible for debts contracted by his wife, even before her marriage, as well as for his own; but he could use her as a mancipium. Hence the Code allowed a proviso to be inserted in the marriage contract, that the wife should not be seized for her husband's prenuptial debts; but enacted that then he was not responsible for her prenuptial debts, and, in any case, that both together were responsible for all debts contracted after marriage. A man might make his wife a settlement by deed of gift, which gave her a life interest in part of his property, and he might reserve to her the right to bequeath it to a favourite child, but she could in no case leave it to her family. Although married she always remained a member of her father's house--she is rarely named wife of A, usually daughter of B, or mother of C.

Divorce was optional with the man, but he had to restore the dowry and, if the wife had borne him children, she had the custody of them. He had then to assign her the income of field, or garden, as well as goods, to maintain herself and children until they grew up. She then shared equally with them in the allowance (and apparently in his estate at his death) and was free to marry again. If she had no children, he returned her the dowry and paid her a sum equivalent to the bride-price, or a mina of silver, if there had been none. The latter is the forfeit usually named in the contract for his repudiation of her.

If she had been a bad wife, the Code allowed him to send her away, while he kept the children and her dowry; or he could degrade her to the position of a slave in his own house, where she would have food and clothing. She might bring an action against him for cruelty and neglect and, if she proved her case, obtain a judicial separation, taking with her her dowry. No other punishment fell on the man. If she did not prove her case, but proved to be a bad wife, she was drowned. If she were left without maintenance during her husband's involuntary absence, she could cohabit with another man, but must return to her husband if he came back, the children of the second union remaining with their own father. If she had maintenance, a breach of the marriage tie was adultery. Wilful desertion by, or exile of, the husband dissolved the marriage, and if he came back he had no claim on her property; possibly not on his own.

As a widow, the wife took her husband's place in the family, living on in his house and bringing up the children. She could only remarry with judicial consent, when the judge was bound to inventory the deceased's estate and hand it over to her and her new husband in trust for the children. They could not alienate a single utensil. If she did not remarry, she lived on in her husband's house and took a child's share on the division of his estate, when the children had grown up. She still retained her dowry and any settlement deeded to her by her husband. This property came to her children. If she had remarried, all her children shared equally in her dowry, but the first husband's gift fell to his children or to her selection among them, if so empowered.

Monogamy was the rule, and a childless wife might give her husband a maid (who was no wife) to bear him children, who were reckoned hers. She remained mistress of her maid and might degrade her to slavery again for insolence, but could not sell her if she had borne her husband children. If the wife did this, the Code did not allow the husband to take a concubine. If she would not, he could do so. The concubine was a wife, though not of the same rank; the first wife had no power over her. A concubine was a free woman, was often dowered for marriage and her children were legitimate. She could only be divorced on the same conditions as a wife. If a wife became a chronic invalid, the husband was bound to maintain her in the home they bad made together, unless she preferred to take her dowry and go back to her father's house; but he was free to remarry. In all these cases the children were legitimate and legal heirs.

There was, of course, no hindrance to a man having children by a slave girl. These children were free, in any case, and their mother could not be sold, though she might be pledged, and she was free on her master's death. These children could be legitimized by their father's acknowledgment before witnesses, and were often adopted. They then ranked equally in sharing their father's estate, but if not adopted, the wife's children divided and took first choice.

Vestal virgins were not supposed to have children, yet they could and often did marry. The Code contemplated that such a wife would give a husband a maid as above. Free women might marry slaves and be dowered for the marriage. The children were free, and at the slave's death the wife took her dowry and half what she and her husband had acquired in wedlock for self and children; the master taking the other half as his slave's heir.

A father had control over his children till their marriage. He had a right to their labour in return for their keep. He might hire them out and receive their wages, pledge them for debt, even sell them outright. Mothers had the same rights in the absence of the father; even elder brothers when both parents were dead. A father had no claim on his married children for support, but they retained a right to inherit on his death.

The daughter was not only in her father's power to be given in marriage, but he might dedicate her to the service of some god as a vestal or a hierodule; or give her as a concubine. She had no choice in these matters, which were often decided in her childhood. A grown-up daughter might wish to become a votary, perhaps in preference to an uncongenial marriage, and it seems that her father could not refuse her wish. In all these cases the father might dower her. If he did not, on his death the brothers were bound to do so, giving her a full child's share if a wife, a concubine or a vestal, but one-third of a child's share if she were a hierodule or a Marduk priestess. The latter had the privilege of exemption from state dues and absolute disposal of her property. All other daughters had only a life interest in their dowry, which reverted to their family, if childless, or went to their children if they had any. A father might, however, execute a deed granting a daughter power to leave her property to a favourite brother or sister. A daughter's estate was usually managed for her by her brothers, but if they did not satisfy her, she could appoint a steward. If she married, her husband managed it.

The son also appears to have received his share on marriage, but did not always then leave his father's house; he might bring his wife there. This was usual in child marriages.

Adoption was very common, especially where the father (or mother) was childless or had seen all his children grow up and marry away. The child was then adopted to care for the parents' old age. This was done by contract, which usually specified what the parent had to leave and what maintenance was expected. The real children, if any, were usually consenting parties to an arrangement which cut off their expectations. They even, in some cases, found the estate for the adopted child who was to relieve them of a care. If the adopted child failed to carry out the filial duty the contract was annulled in the law courts. Slaves were often adopted and if they proved unfilial were reduced to slavery again.

A craftsman often adopted a son to learn the craft. He profited by the son's labour. If he failed to teach his son the craft, that son could prosecute him and get the contract annulled. This was a form of apprenticeship, and it is not clear that the apprentice had any filial relation.

A man who adopted a son, and afterwards married and had a family of his own, could dissolve the contract but must give the adopted child one-third of a child's share in goods, but no real estate. That could only descend in the family to which he had ceased to belong. Vestals frequently adopted daughters, usually other vestals, to care for their old age.

Adoption had to be with consent of the real parents, who usually executed a deed making over the child, who thus ceased to have any claim upon them. But vestals, hierodules, certain palace officials and slaves had no rights over their children and could raise no obstacle. Foundlings and illegitimate children had no parents to object. If the adopted child discovered his true parents and wanted to return to them, his eye or tongue was torn out. An adopted child was a full heir, the contract might even assign him the position of eldest son. Usually he was residuary legatee.

All legitimate children shared equally in the father's estate at his death, reservation being made of a bride-price for an unmarried son, dower for a daughter or property deeded to favourite children by the father. There was no birthright attaching to the position of eldest son, but he usually acted as executor and after considering what each had already received equalized the shares. He even made grants in excess to the others from his own share. When there were two mothers, the two families shared equally in the father's estate until later times when the first family took two-thirds. Daughters, in the absence of sons, had sons' rights. Children also shared their own mother's property, but had no share in that of a stepmother.

A father could disinherit a son in early times without restriction, but the Code insisted upon judicial consent and that only for repeated unfilial conduct. In early times the son who denied his father had his front hair shorn, a slave-mark put on him, and could be sold as a slave; while if he denied his mother he had his front hair shorn, was driven round the city as an example and expelled his home, but not degraded to slavery.

Adultery was punished with the death of both parties by drowning, but if the husband was willing to pardon his wife, the king might intervene to pardon the paramour. For incest with his own mother, both were burned to death; with a stepmother, the man was disinherited; with a daughter, the man was exiled; with a daughter-in-law, he was drowned; with a son's betrothed, he was fined. A wife who for her lover's sake procured her husband's death was gibbeted. A betrothed girl, seduced by her prospective father-in-law, took her dowry and returned to her family, and was free to marry as she chose.

In the criminal law the ruling principle was the lex talionis. Eye for eye, tooth for tooth, limb for limb was the penalty for assault upon an amelu. A sort of symbolic retaliation was the punishment of the offending member, seen in the cutting off the hand that struck a father or stole a trust; in cutting off the breast of a wet-nurse who substituted a changeling for the child entrusted to her; in the loss of the tongue that denied father or mother (in the Elamite contracts the same penalty was inflicted for perjury); in the loss of the eye that pried into forbidden secrets. The loss of the surgeon's hand that caused loss of life or limb or the brander's hand that obliterated a slave's identification mark, are very similar. The slave, who struck a freeman or denied his master, lost an ear, the organ of hearing and symbol of obedience. To bring another into danger of death by false accusation was punished by death. To cause loss of liberty or property by false witness was punished by the penalty the perjurer sought to bring upon another.

The death penalty was freely awarded for theft and other crimes regarded as coming under that head, for theft involving entrance of palace or temple treasury, for illegal purchase from minor or slave, for selling stolen goods or receiving the same, for common theft in the open (in default of multiple restoration) or receiving the same, for false claim to goods, for kidnapping, for assisting or harbouring fugitive slaves, for detaining or appropriating same, for brigandage, for fraudulent sale of drink, for disorderly conduct of tavern, for delegation of personal service, for misappropriating the levy, for oppression of feudal holders, for causing death of a householder by bad building. The manner of death is not specified in these cases. This death penalty was also fixed for such conduct as placed another in danger of death. A specified form of death penalty occurs in the following cases:- gibbeting (on the spot where crime was committed) for burglary, later also for encroaching on the king's highway, for getting a slave-brand obliterated, for procuring husband's death; burning for incest with own mother, for vestal entering or opening tavern, for theft at fire (on the spot); drowning for adultery, rape of betrothed maiden, bigamy, bad conduct as wife, seduction of daughter-in-law.

A curious extension of the talio is the death of creditor's son for his father's having caused the death of debtor's son as mancipium; of builder's son for his father's causing the death of house-owner's son by building the house badly; the death of a man's daughter because her father caused the death of another man's daughter.

The contracts naturally do not concern such criminal cases as the above, as a rule, but marriage contracts do specify death by strangling, drowning, precipitation from a tower or pinnacle of the temple or by the iron sword for a wife's repudiation of her husband. We are quite without evidence as to the executive in all these cases.

Exile was inflicted for incest with a daughter; disinheritance for incest with a stepmother or for repeated unfilial conduct. Sixty strokes of an ox-hide scourge were awarded for a brutal assault on a superior, both being amelu. Branding (perhaps the equivalent of degradation to slavery) was the penalty for slander of a married woman or vestal. Deprivation of office in perpetuity fell upon the corrupt judge. Enslavement befell the extravagant wife and unfilial children. Imprisonment was common, but is not recognized by the Code.

The commonest of all penalties was a fine. This is awarded by the Code for corporal injuries to a muskinu or slave (paid to his master); for damages done to property, for breach of contract. The restoration of goods appropriated, illegally bought or damaged by neglect, was usually accompanied by a fine, giving it the form of multiple restoration. This might be double, treble, fourfold, fivefold, sixfold, tenfold, twelvefold, even thirtyfold, according to the enormity of the offence.

The Code recognized the importance of intention. A man who killed another in a quarrel must swear he did not do so intentionally, and was then only fined according to the rank of the deceased. The Code does not say what would be the penalty of murder, but death is so often awarded where death is caused that we can hardly doubt that the murderer was put to death. If the assault only led to injury and was unintentional, the assailant in a quarrel had to pay the doctor's fees. A brander, induced to remove a slave's identification mark, could swear to his ignorance and was free. The owner of an ox which gored a man on the street was only responsible for damages if, the ox was known by him to be vicious, even if it caused death. If the mancipium died a natural death under the creditor's hand, the creditor was scot free. In ordinary cases responsibility was not demanded for accident or for more than proper care. Poverty excused bigamy on the part of a deserted wife.

On the other hand carelessness and neglect were severely punished, as in the case of the unskilful physician, if it led to loss of life or limb his hands were cut off, a slave had to be replaced, the loss of his eye paid for to half his value; a veterinary surgeon who caused the death of an ox or ass paid quarter value; a builder, whose careless workmanship caused death, lost his life or paid for it by the death of his child, replaced slave or goods, and in any case had to rebuild the house or make good any damages due to defective building and repair the defect as well. The boat-builder had to make good any defect of construction or damage due to it for a year's warranty.

Throughout the Code respect is paid to status.

Suspicion was not enough. The criminal must be taken in the act, e.g. the adulterer, ravisher, &c. A man could not be convicted of theft unless the goods were found in his possession.

In the case of a lawsuit the plaintiff preferred his own plea. There is no trace of professional advocates, but the plea had to be in writing and the notary doubtless assisted in the drafting of it. The judge saw the plea, called the other parties before him and sent for the witnesses. If these were not at hand he might adjourn the case for their production, specifying a time up to six months. Guarantees might be entered into to produce the witnesses on a fixed day. The more important cases, especially those involving life and death, were tried by a bench of judges. With the judges were associated a body of elders, who shared in the decision, but whose exact function is not yet clear. Agreements, declarations and non-contentious cases are usually witnessed by one judge and twelve elders. Parties and witnesses were put on oath. The penalty for the false witness was usually that which would have been awarded the convicted criminal. In matters beyond the knowledge of men, as the guilt or innocence of an alleged wizard or a suspected wife, the ordeal by water was used. The accused jumped into the sacred river, and the innocent swam while the guilty drowned. The accused could clear himself by oath where his own knowledge was alone available. The plaintiff could swear to his loss by brigands, as to goods claimed, the price paid for a slave purchased abroad or the sum due to him. But great stress was laid on the production of written evidence. It was a serious thing to lose a document. The judges might be satisfied of its existence and terms by the evidence of the witnesses to it, and then issue an order that whenever found it should be given up. Contracts annulled were ordered to be broken. The court might go a journey to view the property and even take with them the sacred symbols on which oath was made.

The decision given was embodied in writing, sealed and witnessed by the judges, the elders, witnesses and a scribe. Women might act in all these capacities. The parties swore an oath, embodied in the document, to observe its stipulations. Each took a copy and one was held by the scribe to be stored in the archives.

Appeal to the king was allowed and is well attested. The judges at Babylon seem to have formed a superior court to those of provincial towns, but a defendant might elect to answer the charge before the local court and refuse to plead at Babylon.

Finally, it may be noted that many immoral acts, such as the use of false weights, lying, &c., which could not be brought into court, are severely denounced in the Omen Tablets as likely to bring the offender into "the hand of God" as opposed to "the hand of the king."

The Code of King Hammurabi

Hammurabi

The Law of Babylon

When Anu the Sublime, King of the Anunaki, and Bel, the lord of Heaven and earth, who decreed the fate of the land, assigned to Marduk, the over-ruling son of Ea, God of righteousness, dominion over earthly man, and made him great among the Igigi, they called Babylon by his illustrious name, made it great on earth, and founded an everlasting kingdom in it, whose foundations are laid so solidly as those of heaven and earth; then Anu and Bel called by name me, Hammurabi, the exalted prince, who feared God, to bring about the rule of righteousness in the land, to destroy the wicked and the evil-doers; so that the strong should not harm the weak; so that I should rule over the black-headed people like Shamash, and enlighten the land, to further the well-being of mankind.

Hammurabi, the prince, called of Bel am I, making riches and increase, enriching Nippur and Dur-ilu beyond compare, sublime patron of E-kur; who reestablished Eridu and purified the worship of E-apsu; who conquered the four quarters of the world, made great the name of Babylon, rejoiced the heart of Marduk, his lord who daily pays his devotions in Saggil; the royal scion whom Sin made; who enriched Ur; the humble, the reverent, who brings wealth to Gish-shir-gal; the white king, heard of Shamash, the mighty, who again laid the foundations of Sippara; who clothed the gravestones of Malkat with green; who made E-babbar great, which is like the heavens, the warrior who guarded Larsa and renewed E-babbar, with Shamash as his helper; the lord who granted new life to Uruk, who brought plenteous water to its inhabitants, raised the head of E-anna, and perfected the beauty of Anu and Nana; shield of the land, who reunited the scattered inhabitants of Isin; who richly endowed E-gal-mach; the protecting king of the city, brother of the god Zamama; who firmly founded the farms of Kish, crowned E-me-te-ursag with glory, redoubled the great holy treasures of Nana, managed the temple of Harsag-kalama; the grave of the enemy, whose help brought about the victory; who increased the power of Cuthah; made all glorious in E-shidlam, the black steer, who gored the enemy; beloved of the god Nebo, who rejoiced the inhabitants of Borsippa, the Sublime; who is indefatigable for E-zida; the divine king of the city; the White, Wise; who broadened the fields of Dilbat, who heaped up the harvests for Urash; the Mighty, the lord to whom come scepter and crown, with which he clothes himself; the Elect of Ma-ma; who fixed the temple bounds of Kesh, who made rich the holy feasts of Nin-tu; the provident, solicitous, who provided food and drink for Lagash and Girsu, who provided large sacrificial offerings for the temple of Ningirsu; who captured the enemy, the Elect of the oracle who fulfilled the prediction of Hallab, who rejoiced the heart of Anunit; the pure prince, whose prayer is accepted by Adad; who satisfied the heart of Adad, the warrior, in Karkar, who restored the vessels for worship in E-ud-gal-gal; the king who granted life to the city of Adab; the guide of E-mach; the princely king of the city, the irresistible warrior, who granted life to the inhabitants of Mashkanshabri, and brought abundance to the temple of Shidlam; the White, Potent, who penetrated the secret cave of the bandits, saved the inhabitants of Malka from misfortune, and fixed their home fast in wealth; who established pure sacrificial gifts for Ea and Dam-gal-nun-na, who made his kingdom everlastingly great; the princely king of the city, who subjected the districts on the Ud-kib-nun-na Canal to the sway of Dagon, his Creator; who spared the inhabitants of Mera and Tutul; the sublime prince, who makes the face of Ninni shine; who presents holy meals to the divinity of Nin-a-zu, who cared for its inhabitants in their need, provided a portion for them in Babylon in peace; the shepherd of the oppressed and of the slaves; whose deeds find favor before Anunit, who provided for Anunit in the temple of Dumash in the suburb of Agade; who recognizes the right, who rules by law; who gave back to the city of Ashur its protecting god; who let the name of Ishtar of Nineveh remain in E-mish-mish; the Sublime, who humbles himself before the great gods; successor of Sumula-il; the mighty son of Sin-muballit; the royal scion of Eternity; the mighty monarch, the sun of Babylon, whose rays shed light over the land of Sumer and Akkad; the king, obeyed by the four quarters of the world; Beloved of Ninni, am I.

When Marduk sent me to rule over men, to give the protection of right to the land, I did right and righteousness in . . . , and brought about the well-being of the oppressed.

THE CODES

1. If any one ensnare another, putting a ban upon him, but he can not prove it, then he that ensnared him shall be put to death.

2. If any one bring an accusation against a man, and the accused go to the river and leap into the river, if he sink in the river his

accuser shall take possession of his house. But if the river prove that the accused is not guilty, and he escape unhurt, then he who had brought the accusation shall be put to death, while he who leaped into the river shall take possession of the house that had belonged to his accuser.

3. If any one bring an accusation of any crime before the elders, and does not prove what he has charged, he shall, if it be a capital offense charged, be put to death.

4. If he satisfy the elders to impose a fine of grain or money, he shall receive the fine that the action produces.

5. If a judge try a case, reach a decision, and present his judgment in writing; if later error shall appear in his decision, and it be through his own fault, then he shall pay twelve times the fine set by him in the case, and he shall be publicly removed from the judge's bench, and never again shall he sit there to render judgement.

6. If any one steal the property of a temple or of the court, he shall be put to death, and also the one who receives the stolen thing from him shall be put to death.

7. If any one buy from the son or the slave of another man, without witnesses or a contract, silver or gold, a male or female slave, an ox or a sheep, an ass or anything, or if he take it in charge, he is considered a thief and shall be put to death.

8. If any one steal cattle or sheep, or an ass, or a pig or a goat, if it belong to a god or to the court, the thief shall pay thirtyfold

therefor; if they belonged to a freed man of the king he shall pay tenfold; if the thief has nothing with which to pay he shall be put to death.

9. If any one lose an article, and find it in the possession of another: if the person in whose possession the thing is found say "A merchant sold it to me, I paid for it before witnesses," and if the owner of the thing say, "I will bring witnesses who know my property," then shall the purchaser bring the merchant who sold it to him, and the witnesses before whom he bought it, and the owner shall bring witnesses who can identify his property. The judge shall examine their testimony--both of the witnesses before whom the price was paid, and of the witnesses who identify the lost article on oath. The merchant is then proved to be a thief and shall be put to death. The owner of the lost article receives his property, and he who bought it receives the money he paid from the estate of the merchant.

10. If the purchaser does not bring the merchant and the witnesses before whom he bought the article, but its owner bring witnesses who identify it, then the buyer is the thief and shall be put to death, and the owner receives the lost article.

11. If the owner do not bring witnesses to identify the lost article, he is an evil-doer, he has traduced, and shall be put to death.

12. If the witnesses be not at hand, then shall the judge set a limit, at the expiration of six months. If his witnesses have not appeared within the six months, he is an evil-doer, and shall bear the fine of the pending case.

14. If any one steal the minor son of another, he shall be put to death.

15. If any one take a male or female slave of the court, or a male or female slave of a freed man, outside the city gates, he shall be put to death.

16. If any one receive into his house a runaway male or female slave of the court, or of a freedman, and does not bring it out at the public proclamation of the major domus, the master of the house shall be put to death.

17. If any one find runaway male or female slaves in the open country and bring them to their masters, the master of the slaves shall pay him two shekels of silver.

18. If the slave will not give the name of the master, the finder shall bring him to the palace; a further investigation must follow, and the slave shall be returned to his master.

19. If he hold the slaves in his house, and they are caught there, he shall be put to death.

20. If the slave that he caught run away from him, then shall he swear to the owners of the slave, and he is free of all blame.

21. If any one break a hole into a house (break in to steal), he shall be put to death before that hole and be buried.

22. If any one is committing a robbery and is caught, then he shall be put to death.

23. If the robber is not caught, then shall he who was robbed claim under oath the amount of his loss; then shall the community, and . . . on whose ground and territory and in whose domain it was compensate him for the goods stolen.

24. If persons are stolen, then shall the community and . . . pay one mina of silver to their relatives.

25. If fire break out in a house, and some one who comes to put it out cast his eye upon the property of the owner of the house, and take the property of the master of the house, he shall be thrown into that self-same fire.

26. If a chieftain or a man (common soldier), who has been ordered to go upon the king's highway for war does not go, but hires a mercenary, if he withholds the compensation, then shall this officer or man be put to death, and he who represented him shall take possession of his house.

27. If a chieftain or man be caught in the misfortune of the king (captured in battle), and if his fields and garden be given to another and he take possession, if he return and reaches his place, his field and garden shall be returned to him, he shall take it over again.

28. If a chieftain or a man be caught in the misfortune of a king, if his son is able to enter into possession, then the field and garden shall be given to him, he shall take over the fee of his father.

29. If his son is still young, and can not take possession, a third of the field and garden shall be given to his mother, and she shall bring him up.

30. If a chieftain or a man leave his house, garden, and field and hires it out, and some one else takes possession of his house, garden, and field and uses it for three years: if the first owner return and claims his house, garden, and field, it shall not be given to him, but he who has taken possession of it and used it shall continue to use it.

31. If he hire it out for one year and then return, the house, garden, and field shall be given back to him, and he shall take it over again.

32. If a chieftain or a man is captured on the "Way of the King" (in war), and a merchant buy him free, and bring him back to his place; if he have the means in his house to buy his freedom, he shall buy himself free: if he have nothing in his house with which to buy himself free, he shall be bought free by the temple of his community; if there be nothing in the temple with which to buy him free, the court shall buy his freedom. His field, garden, and house shall not be given for the purchase of his freedom.

33. If a . . . or a . . . enter himself as withdrawn from the "Way of the King," and send a mercenary as substitute, but withdraw him, then the . . . or . . . shall be put to death.

34. If a . . . or a . . . harm the property of a captain, injure the captain, or take away from the captain a gift presented to him by the king, then the . . . or . . . shall be put to death.

35. If any one buy the cattle or sheep which the king has given to chieftains from him, he loses his money.

36. The field, garden, and house of a chieftain, of a man, or of one subject to quit-rent, can not be sold.

37. If any one buy the field, garden, and house of a chieftain, man, or one subject to quit-rent, his contract tablet of sale shall be broken (declared invalid) and he loses his money. The field, garden, and house return to their owners.

38. A chieftain, man, or one subject to quit-rent can not assign his tenure of field, house, and garden to his wife or daughter, nor can he assign it for a debt.

39. He may, however, assign a field, garden, or house which he has bought, and holds as property, to his wife or daughter or give it for debt.

40. He may sell field, garden, and house to a merchant (royal agents) or to any other public official, the buyer holding field, house, and garden for its usufruct.

41. If any one fence in the field, garden, and house of a chieftain, man, or one subject to quit-rent, furnishing the palings therefor; if the chieftain, man, or one subject to quit-rent return to field, garden,

and house, the palings which were given to him become his property.

42. If any one take over a field to till it, and obtain no harvest therefrom, it must be proved that he did no work on the field, and he must deliver grain, just as his neighbor raised, to the owner of the field.

43. If he do not till the field, but let it lie fallow, he shall give grain like his neighbor's to the owner of the field, and the field which he let lie fallow he must plow and sow and return to its owner.

44. If any one take over a waste-lying field to make it arable, but is lazy, and does not make it arable, he shall plow the fallow field in the fourth year, harrow it and till it, and give it back to its owner, and for each ten gan (a measure of area) ten gur of grain shall be paid.

45. If a man rent his field for tillage for a fixed rental, and receive the rent of his field, but bad weather come and destroy the harvest, the injury falls upon the tiller of the soil.

46. If he do not receive a fixed rental for his field, but lets it on half or third shares of the harvest, the grain on the field shall be divided proportionately between the tiller and the owner.

47. If the tiller, because he did not succeed in the first year, has had the soil tilled by others, the owner may raise no objection; the field has been cultivated and he receives the harvest according to agreement.

48. If any one owe a debt for a loan, and a storm prostrates the grain, or the harvest fail, or the grain does not grow for lack of water; in that year he need not give his creditor any grain, he washes his debt-tablet in water and pays no rent for this year.

49. If any one take money from a merchant, and give the merchant a field tillable for corn or sesame and order him to plant corn or sesame in the field, and to harvest the crop; if the cultivator plant corn or sesame in the field, at the harvest the corn or sesame that is in the field shall belong to the owner of the field and he shall pay corn as rent, for the money he received from the merchant, and the livelihood of the cultivator shall he give to the merchant.

50. If he give a cultivated corn-field or a cultivated sesame-field, the corn or sesame in the field shall belong to the owner of the field, and he shall return the money to the merchant as rent.

51. If he have no money to repay, then he shall pay in corn or sesame in place of the money as rent for what he received from the merchant, according to the royal tariff.

52. If the cultivator do not plant corn or sesame in the field, the debtor's contract is not weakened.

53. If any one be too lazy to keep his dam in proper condition, and does not so keep it; if then the dam break and all the fields be flooded, then shall he in whose dam the break occurred be sold for money, and the money shall replace the corn which he has caused to be ruined.

54. If he be not able to replace the corn, then he and his possessions shall be divided among the farmers whose corn he has flooded.

55. If any one open his ditches to water his crop, but is careless, and the water flood the field of his neighbor, then he shall pay his neighbor corn for his loss.

56. If a man let in the water, and the water overflow the plantation of his neighbor, he shall pay ten gur of corn for every ten gan of land.

57. If a shepherd, without the permission of the owner of the field, and without the knowledge of the owner of the sheep, lets the sheep into a field to graze, then the owner of the field shall harvest his crop, and the shepherd, who had pastured his flock there without permission of the owner of the field, shall pay to the owner twenty gur of corn for every ten gan.

58. If after the flocks have left the pasture and been shut up in the common fold at the city gate, any shepherd let them into a field and they graze there, this shepherd shall take possession of the field which he has allowed to be grazed on, and at the harvest he must pay sixty gur of corn for every ten gan.

59. If any man, without the knowledge of the owner of a garden, fell a tree in a garden he shall pay half a mina in money.

60. If any one give over a field to a gardener, for him to plant it as a garden, if he work at it, and care for it for four years, in the fifth

year the owner and the gardener shall divide it, the owner taking his part in charge.

61. If the gardener has not completed the planting of the field, leaving one part unused, this shall be assigned to him as his.

62. If he do not plant the field that was given over to him as a garden, if it be arable land (for corn or sesame) the gardener shall pay the owner the produce of the field for the years that he let it lie fallow, according to the product of neighboring fields, put the field in arable condition and return it to its owner.

63. If he transform waste land into arable fields and return it to its owner, the latter shall pay him for one year ten gur for ten gan.

64. If any one hand over his garden to a gardener to work, the gardener shall pay to its owner two-thirds of the produce of the garden, for so long as he has it in possession, and the other third shall he keep.

65. If the gardener do not work in the garden and the product fall off, the gardener shall pay in proportion to other neighboring gardens. [Here a portion of the text is missing, apparently comprising thirty-four paragraphs.]

100. . . . interest for the money, as much as he has received, he shall give a note therefor, and on the day, when they settle, pay to the merchant.

101. If there are no mercantile arrangements in the place whither he went, he shall leave the entire amount of money which he received with the broker to give to the merchant.

102. If a merchant entrust money to an agent (broker) for some investment, and the broker suffer a loss in the place to which he goes, he shall make good the capital to the merchant.

103. If, while on the journey, an enemy take away from him anything that he had, the broker shall swear by God and be free of obligation.

104. If a merchant give an agent corn, wool, oil, or any other goods to transport, the agent shall give a receipt for the amount, and compensate the merchant therefor. Then he shall obtain a receipt form the merchant for the money that he gives the merchant.

105. If the agent is careless, and does not take a receipt for the money which he gave the merchant, he can not consider the unreceipted money as his own.

106. If the agent accept money from the merchant, but have a quarrel with the merchant (denying the receipt), then shall the merchant swear before God and witnesses that he has given this money to the agent, and the agent shall pay him three times the sum.

107. If the merchant cheat the agent, in that as the latter has returned to him all that had been given him, but the merchant denies the receipt of what had been returned to him, then shall this agent convict the merchant before God and the judges, and if he still deny

receiving what the agent had given him shall pay six times the sum to the agent.

108. If a tavern-keeper (feminine) does not accept corn according to gross weight in payment of drink, but takes money, and the price of the drink is less than that of the corn, she shall be convicted and thrown into the water.

109. If conspirators meet in the house of a tavern-keeper, and these conspirators are not captured and delivered to the court, the tavern-keeper shall be put to death.

110. If a "sister of a god" open a tavern, or enter a tavern to drink, then shall this woman be burned to death.

111. If an inn-keeper furnish sixty ka of usakani-drink to . . . she shall receive fifty ka of corn at the harvest.

112. If any one be on a journey and entrust silver, gold, precious stones, or any movable property to another, and wish to recover it from him; if the latter do not bring all of the property to the appointed place, but appropriate it to his own use, then shall this man, who did not bring the property to hand it over, be convicted, and he shall pay fivefold for all that had been entrusted to him.

113. If any one have consignment of corn or money, and he take from the granary or box without the knowledge of the owner, then shall he who took corn without the knowledge of the owner out of the granary or money out of the box be legally convicted, and repay

the corn he has taken. And he shall lose whatever commission was paid to him, or due him.

114. If a man have no claim on another for corn and money, and try to demand it by force, he shall pay one-third of a mina of silver in every case.

115. If any one have a claim for corn or money upon another and imprison him; if the prisoner die in prison a natural death, the case shall go no further.

116. If the prisoner die in prison from blows or maltreatment, the master of the prisoner shall convict the merchant before the judge. If he was a free-born man, the son of the merchant shall be put to death; if it was a slave, he shall pay one-third of a mina of gold, and all that the master of the prisoner gave he shall forfeit.

117. If any one fail to meet a claim for debt, and sell himself, his wife, his son, and daughter for money or give them away to forced labor: they shall work for three years in the house of the man who bought them, or the proprietor, and in the fourth year they shall be set free.

118. If he give a male or female slave away for forced labor, and the merchant sublease them, or sell them for money, no objection can be raised.

119. If any one fail to meet a claim for debt, and he sell the maid servant who has borne him children, for money, the money which

the merchant has paid shall be repaid to him by the owner of the slave and she shall be freed.

120. If any one store corn for safe keeping in another person's house, and any harm happen to the corn in storage, or if the owner of the house open the granary and take some of the corn, or if especially he deny that the corn was stored in his house: then the owner of the corn shall claim his corn before God (on oath), and the owner of the house shall pay its owner for all of the corn that he took.

121. If any one store corn in another man's house he shall pay him storage at the rate of one gur for every five ka of corn per year.

122. If any one give another silver, gold, or anything else to keep, he shall show everything to some witness, draw up a contract, and then hand it over for safe keeping.

123. If he turn it over for safe keeping without witness or contract, and if he to whom it was given deny it, then he has no legitimate claim.

124. If any one deliver silver, gold, or anything else to another for safe keeping, before a witness, but he deny it, he shall be brought before a judge, and all that he has denied he shall pay in full.

125. If any one place his property with another for safe keeping, and there, either through thieves or robbers, his property and the property of the other man be lost, the owner of the house, through whose neglect the loss took place, shall compensate the owner for all

that was given to him in charge. But the owner of the house shall try to follow up and recover his property, and take it away from the thief.

126. If any one who has not lost his goods state that they have been lost, and make false claims: if he claim his goods and amount of injury before God, even though he has not lost them, he shall be fully compensated for all his loss claimed. (I.e., the oath is all that is needed.)

127. If any one "point the finger" (slander) at a sister of a god or the wife of any one, and can not prove it, this man shall be taken before the judges and his brow shall be marked. (by cutting the skin, or perhaps hair.)

128. If a man take a woman to wife, but have no intercourse with her, this woman is no wife to him.

129. If a man's wife be surprised (in flagrante delicto) with another man, both shall be tied and thrown into the water, but the husband may pardon his wife and the king his slaves.

130. If a man violate the wife (betrothed or child-wife) of another man, who has never known a man, and still lives in her father's house, and sleep with her and be surprised, this man shall be put to death, but the wife is blameless.

131. If a man bring a charge against one's wife, but she is not surprised with another man, she must take an oath and then may return to her house.

132. If the "finger is pointed" at a man's wife about another man, but she is not caught sleeping with the other man, she shall jump into the river for her husband.

133. If a man is taken prisoner in war, and there is a sustenance in his house, but his wife leave house and court, and go to another house: because this wife did not keep her court, and went to another house, she shall be judicially condemned and thrown into the water.

134. If any one be captured in war and there is not sustenance in his house, if then his wife go to another house this woman shall be held blameless.

135. If a man be taken prisoner in war and there be no sustenance in his house and his wife go to another house and bear children; and if later her husband return and come to his home: then this wife shall return to her husband, but the children follow their father.

136. If any one leave his house, run away, and then his wife go to another house, if then he return, and wishes to take his wife back: because he fled from his home and ran away, the wife of this runaway shall not return to her husband.

137. If a man wish to separate from a woman who has borne him children, or from his wife who has borne him children: then he shall give that wife her dowry, and a part of the usufruct of field, garden, and property, so that she can rear her children. When she has brought up her children, a portion of all that is given to the children, equal as

that of one son, shall be given to her. She may then marry the man of her heart.

138. If a man wishes to separate from his wife who has borne him no children, he shall give her the amount of her purchase money and the dowry which she brought from her father's house, and let her go.

139. If there was no purchase price he shall give her one mina of gold as a gift of release.

140. If he be a freed man he shall give her one-third of a mina of gold.

141. If a man's wife, who lives in his house, wishes to leave it, plunges into debt, tries to ruin her house, neglects her husband, and is judicially convicted: if her husband offer her release, she may go on her way, and he gives her nothing as a gift of release. If her husband does not wish to release her, and if he take another wife, she shall remain as servant in her husband's house.

142. If a woman quarrel with her husband, and say: "You are not congenial to me," the reasons for her prejudice must be presented. If she is guiltless, and there is no fault on her part, but he leaves and neglects her, then no guilt attaches to this woman, she shall take her dowry and go back to her father's house.

143. If she is not innocent, but leaves her husband, and ruins her house, neglecting her husband, this woman shall be cast into the water.

144. If a man take a wife and this woman give her husband a maid-servant, and she bear him children, but this man wishes to take another wife, this shall not be permitted to him; he shall not take a second wife.

145. If a man take a wife, and she bear him no children, and he intend to take another wife: if he take this second wife, and bring her into the house, this second wife shall not be allowed equality with his wife.

146. If a man take a wife and she give this man a maid-servant as wife and she bear him children, and then this maid assume equality with the wife: because she has borne him children her master shall not sell her for money, but he may keep her as a slave, reckoning her among the maid-servants.

147. If she have not borne him children, then her mistress may sell her for money.

148. If a man take a wife, and she be seized by disease, if he then desire to take a second wife he shall not put away his wife, who has been attacked by disease, but he shall keep her in the house which he has built and support her so long as she lives.

149. If this woman does not wish to remain in her husband's house, then he shall compensate her for the dowry that she brought with her from her father's house, and she may go.

150. If a man give his wife a field, garden, and house and a deed therefor, if then after the death of her husband the sons raise no

claim, then the mother may bequeath all to one of her sons whom she prefers, and need leave nothing to his brothers.

151. If a woman who lived in a man's house made an agreement with her husband, that no creditor can arrest her, and has given a document therefor: if that man, before he married that woman, had a debt, the creditor can not hold the woman for it. But if the woman, before she entered the man's house, had contracted a debt, her creditor can not arrest her husband therefor.

152. If after the woman had entered the man's house, both contracted a debt, both must pay the merchant.

153. If the wife of one man on account of another man has their mates (her husband and the other man's wife) murdered, both of them shall be impaled.

154. If a man be guilty of incest with his daughter, he shall be driven from the place (exiled).

155. If a man betroth a girl to his son, and his son have intercourse with her, but he (the father) afterward defile her, and be surprised, then he shall be bound and cast into the water (drowned).

156. If a man betroth a girl to his son, but his son has not known her, and if then he defile her, he shall pay her half a gold mina, and compensate her for all that she brought out of her father's house. She may marry the man of her heart.

157. If any one be guilty of incest with his mother after his father, both shall be burned.

158. If any one be surprised after his father with his chief wife, who has borne children, he shall be driven out of his father's house.

159. If any one, who has brought chattels into his father-in-law's house, and has paid the purchase-money, looks for another wife, and says to his father-in-law: "I do not want your daughter," the girl's father may keep all that he had brought.

160. If a man bring chattels into the house of his father-in-law, and pay the "purchase price" (for his wife): if then the father of the girl say: "I will not give you my daughter," he shall give him back all that he brought with him.

161. If a man bring chattels into his father-in-law's house and pay the "purchase price," if then his friend slander him, and his father-in-law say to the young husband: "You shall not marry my daughter," the he shall give back to him undiminished all that he had brought with him; but his wife shall not be married to the friend.

162. If a man marry a woman, and she bear sons to him; if then this woman die, then shall her father have no claim on her dowry; this belongs to her sons.

163. If a man marry a woman and she bear him no sons; if then this woman die, if the "purchase price" which he had paid into the house of his father-in-law is repaid to him, her husband shall have no claim upon the dowry of this woman; it belongs to her father's house.

164. If his father-in-law do not pay back to him the amount of the "purchase price" he may subtract the amount of the "Purchase price" from the dowry, and then pay the remainder to her father's house.

165. If a man give to one of his sons whom he prefers a field, garden, and house, and a deed therefor: if later the father die, and the brothers divide the estate, then they shall first give him the present of his father, and he shall accept it; and the rest of the paternal property shall they divide.

166. If a man take wives for his son, but take no wife for his minor son, and if then he die: if the sons divide the estate, they shall set aside besides his portion the money for the "purchase price" for the minor brother who had taken no wife as yet, and secure a wife for him.

167. If a man marry a wife and she bear him children: if this wife die and he then take another wife and she bear him children: if then the father die, the sons must not partition the estate according to the mothers, they shall divide the dowries of their mothers only in this way; the paternal estate they shall divide equally with one another.

168. If a man wish to put his son out of his house, and declare before the judge: "I want to put my son out," then the judge shall examine into his reasons. If the son be guilty of no great fault, for which he can be rightfully put out, the father shall not put him out.

169. If he be guilty of a grave fault, which should rightfully deprive him of the filial relationship, the father shall forgive him the first time; but if he be guilty of a grave fault a second time the father may deprive his son of all filial relation.

170. If his wife bear sons to a man, or his maid-servant have borne sons, and the father while still living says to the children whom his maid-servant has borne: "My sons," and he count them with the sons of his wife; if then the father die, then the sons of the wife and of the maid-servant shall divide the paternal property in common. The son of the wife is to partition and choose.

171. If, however, the father while still living did not say to the sons of the maid-servant: "My sons," and then the father dies, then the sons of the maid-servant shall not share with the sons of the wife, but the freedom of the maid and her sons shall be granted. The sons of the wife shall have no right to enslave the sons of the maid; the wife shall take her dowry (from her father), and the gift that her husband gave her and deeded to her (separate from dowry, or the purchase-money paid her father), and live in the home of her husband: so long as she lives she shall use it, it shall not be sold for money. Whatever she leaves shall belong to her children.

172. If her husband made her no gift, she shall be compensated for her gift, and she shall receive a portion from the estate of her husband, equal to that of one child. If her sons oppress her, to force her out of the house, the judge shall examine into the matter, and if the sons are at fault the woman shall not leave her husband's house.

If the woman desire to leave the house, she must leave to her sons the gift which her husband gave her, but she may take the dowry of her father's house. Then she may marry the man of her heart.

173. If this woman bear sons to her second husband, in the place to which she went, and then die, her earlier and later sons shall divide the dowry between them.

174. If she bear no sons to her second husband, the sons of her first husband shall have the dowry.

175. If a State slave or the slave of a freed man marry the daughter of a free man, and children are born, the master of the slave shall have no right to enslave the children of the free.

176. If, however, a State slave or the slave of a freed man marry a man's daughter, and after he marries her she bring a dowry from a father's house, if then they both enjoy it and found a household, and accumulate means, if then the slave die, then she who was free born may take her dowry, and all that her husband and she had earned; she shall divide them into two parts, one-half the master for the slave shall take, and the other half shall the free-born woman take for her children. If the free-born woman had no gift she shall take all that her husband and she had earned and divide it into two parts; and the master of the slave shall take one-half and she shall take the other for her children.

177. If a widow, whose children are not grown, wishes to enter another house (remarry), she shall not enter it without the knowledge

of the judge. If she enter another house the judge shall examine the state of the house of her first husband. Then the house of her first husband shall be entrusted to the second husband and the woman herself as managers. And a record must be made thereof. She shall keep the house in order, bring up the children, and not sell the household utensils. He who buys the utensils of the children of a widow shall lose his money, and the goods shall return to their owners.

178. If a "devoted woman" or a prostitute to whom her father has given a dowry and a deed therefor, but if in this deed it is not stated that she may bequeath it as she pleases, and has not explicitly stated that she has the right of disposal; if then her father die, then her brothers shall hold her field and garden, and give her corn, oil, and milk according to her portion, and satisfy her. If her brothers do not give her corn, oil, and milk according to her share, then her field and garden shall support her. She shall have the usufruct of field and garden and all that her father gave her so long as she lives, but she can not sell or assign it to others. Her position of inheritance belongs to her brothers.

179. If a "sister of a god," or a prostitute, receive a gift from her father, and a deed in which it has been explicitly stated that she may dispose of it as she pleases, and give her complete disposition thereof: if then her father die, then she may leave her property to whomsoever she pleases. Her brothers can raise no claim thereto.

180. If a father give a present to his daughter--either marriageable or a prostitute unmarriageable)--and then die, then she

is to receive a portion as a child from the paternal estate, and enjoy its usufruct so long as she lives. Her estate belongs to her brothers.

181. If a father devote a temple-maid or temple-virgin to God and give her no present: if then the father die, she shall receive the third of a child's portion from the inheritance of her father's house, and enjoy its usufruct so long as she lives. Her estate belongs to her brothers.

182. If a father devote his daughter as a wife of Mardi of Babylon (as in 181), and give her no present, nor a deed; if then her father die, then shall she receive one-third of her portion as a child of her father's house from her brothers, but Marduk may leave her estate to whomsoever she wishes.

183. If a man give his daughter by a concubine a dowry, and a husband, and a deed; if then her father die, she shall receive no portion from the paternal estate.

184. If a man do not give a dowry to his daughter by a concubine, and no husband; if then her father die, her brother shall give her a dowry according to her father's wealth and secure a husband for her.

185. If a man adopt a child and to his name as son, and rear him, this grown son can not be demanded back again.

186. If a man adopt a son, and if after he has taken him he injure his foster father and mother, then this adopted son shall return to his father's house.

187. The son of a paramour in the palace service, or of a prostitute, can not be demanded back.

188. If an artizan has undertaken to rear a child and teaches him his craft, he can not be demanded back.

189. If he has not taught him his craft, this adopted son may return to his father's house.

190. If a man does not maintain a child that he has adopted as a son and reared with his other children, then his adopted son may return to his father's house.

191. If a man, who had adopted a son and reared him, founded a household, and had children, wish to put this adopted son out, then this son shall not simply go his way. His adoptive father shall give him of his wealth one-third of a child's portion, and then he may go. He shall not give him of the field, garden, and house.

192. If a son of a paramour or a prostitute say to his adoptive father or mother: "You are not my father, or my mother," his tongue shall be cut off.

193. If the son of a paramour or a prostitute desire his father's house, and desert his adoptive father and adoptive mother, and goes to his father's house, then shall his eye be put out.

194. If a man give his child to a nurse and the child die in her hands, but the nurse unbeknown to the father and mother nurse another child, then they shall convict her of having nursed another

child without the knowledge of the father and mother and her breasts shall be cut off.

195. If a son strike his father, his hands shall be hewn off.

196. If a man put out the eye of another man, his eye shall be put out. [An eye for an eye]

197. If he break another man's bone, his bone shall be broken.

198. If he put out the eye of a freed man, or break the bone of a freed man, he shall pay one gold mina.

199. If he put out the eye of a man's slave, or break the bone of a man's slave, he shall pay one-half of its value.

200. If a man knock out the teeth of his equal, his teeth shall be knocked out. [A tooth for a tooth]

201. If he knock out the teeth of a freed man, he shall pay one-third of a gold mina.

202. If any one strike the body of a man higher in rank than he, he shall receive sixty blows with an ox-whip in public.

203. If a free-born man strike the body of another free-born man or equal rank, he shall pay one gold mina.

204. If a freed man strike the body of another freed man, he shall pay ten shekels in money.

205. If the slave of a freed man strike the body of a freed man, his ear shall be cut off.

206. If during a quarrel one man strike another and wound him, then he shall swear, "I did not injure him wittingly," and pay the physicians.

207. If the man die of his wound, he shall swear similarly, and if he (the deceased) was a free-born man, he shall pay half a mina in money.

208. If he was a freed man, he shall pay one-third of a mina.

209. If a man strike a free-born woman so that she lose her unborn child, he shall pay ten shekels for her loss.

210. If the woman die, his daughter shall be put to death.

211. If a woman of the free class lose her child by a blow, he shall pay five shekels in money.

212. If this woman die, he shall pay half a mina.

213. If he strike the maid-servant of a man, and she lose her child, he shall pay two shekels in money.

214. If this maid-servant die, he shall pay one-third of a mina.

215. If a physician make a large incision with an operating knife and cure it, or if he open a tumor (over the eye) with an operating knife, and saves the eye, he shall receive ten shekels in money.

216. If the patient be a freed man, he receives five shekels.

217. If he be the slave of some one, his owner shall give the physician two shekels.

218. If a physician make a large incision with the operating knife, and kill him, or open a tumor with the operating knife, and cut out the eye, his hands shall be cut off.

219. If a physician make a large incision in the slave of a freed man, and kill him, he shall replace the slave with another slave.

220. If he had opened a tumor with the operating knife, and put out his eye, he shall pay half his value.

221. If a physician heal the broken bone or diseased soft part of a man, the patient shall pay the physician five shekels in money.

222. If he were a freed man he shall pay three shekels.

223. If he were a slave his owner shall pay the physician two shekels.

224. If a veterinary surgeon perform a serious operation on an ass or an ox, and cure it, the owner shall pay the surgeon one-sixth of a shekel as a fee.

225. If he perform a serious operation on an ass or ox, and kill it, he shall pay the owner one-fourth of its value.

226. If a barber, without the knowledge of his master, cut the sign of a slave on a slave not to be sold, the hands of this barber shall be cut off.

227. If any one deceive a barber, and have him mark a slave not for sale with the sign of a slave, he shall be put to death, and buried in his house. The barber shall swear: "I did not mark him wittingly," and shall be guiltless.

228. If a builder build a house for some one and complete it, he shall give him a fee of two shekels in money for each sar of surface.

229 If a builder build a house for some one, and does not construct it properly, and the house which he built fall in and kill its owner, then that builder shall be put to death.

230. If it kill the son of the owner the son of that builder shall be put to death.

231. If it kill a slave of the owner, then he shall pay slave for slave to the owner of the house.

232. If it ruin goods, he shall make compensation for all that has been ruined, and inasmuch as he did not construct properly this house which he built and it fell, he shall re-erect the house from his own means.

233. If a builder build a house for some one, even though he has not yet completed it; if then the walls seem toppling, the builder must make the walls solid from his own means.

234. If a shipbuilder build a boat of sixty gur for a man, he shall pay him a fee of two shekels in money.

235. If a shipbuilder build a boat for some one, and do not make it tight, if during that same year that boat is sent away and suffers injury, the shipbuilder shall take the boat apart and put it together tight at his own expense. The tight boat he shall give to the boat owner.

236. If a man rent his boat to a sailor, and the sailor is careless, and the boat is wrecked or goes aground, the sailor shall give the owner of the boat another boat as compensation.

237. If a man hire a sailor and his boat, and provide it with corn, clothing, oil and dates, and other things of the kind needed for fitting it: if the sailor is careless, the boat is wrecked, and its contents ruined, then the sailor shall compensate for the boat which was wrecked and all in it that he ruined.

238. If a sailor wreck any one's ship, but saves it, he shall pay the half of its value in money.

239. If a man hire a sailor, he shall pay him six gur of corn per year.

240. If a merchantman run against a ferryboat, and wreck it, the master of the ship that was wrecked shall seek justice before God; the master of the merchantman, which wrecked the ferryboat, must compensate the owner for the boat and all that he ruined.

241. If any one impresses an ox for forced labor, he shall pay one-third of a mina in money.

242. If any one hire oxen for a year, he shall pay four gur of corn for plow-oxen.

243. As rent of herd cattle he shall pay three gur of corn to the owner.

244. If any one hire an ox or an ass, and a lion kill it in the field, the loss is upon its owner.

245. If any one hire oxen, and kill them by bad treatment or blows, he shall compensate the owner, oxen for oxen.

246. If a man hire an ox, and he break its leg or cut the ligament of its neck, he shall compensate the owner with ox for ox.

247. If any one hire an ox, and put out its eye, he shall pay the owner one-half of its value.

248. If any one hire an ox, and break off a horn, or cut off its tail, or hurt its muzzle, he shall pay one-fourth of its value in money.

249. If any one hire an ox, and God strike it that it die, the man who hired it shall swear by God and be considered guiltless.

250. If while an ox is passing on the street (market) some one push it, and kill it, the owner can set up no claim in the suit (against the hirer).

251. If an ox be a goring ox, and it shown that he is a gorer, and he do not bind his horns, or fasten the ox up, and the ox gore a free-born man and kill him, the owner shall pay one-half a mina in money.

252. If he kill a man's slave, he shall pay one-third of a mina.

253. If any one agree with another to tend his field, give him seed, entrust a yoke of oxen to him, and bind him to cultivate the field, if he steal the corn or plants, and take them for himself, his hands shall be hewn off.

254. If he take the seed-corn for himself, and do not use the yoke of oxen, he shall compensate him for the amount of the seed-corn.

255. If he sublet the man's yoke of oxen or steal the seed-corn, planting nothing in the field, he shall be convicted, and for each one hundred gan he shall pay sixty gur of corn.

256. If his community will not pay for him, then he shall be placed in that field with the cattle (at work).

257. If any one hire a field laborer, he shall pay him eight gur of corn per year.

258. If any one hire an ox-driver, he shall pay him six gur of corn per year.

259. If any one steal a water-wheel from the field, he shall pay five shekels in money to its owner.

260. If any one steal a shadduf (used to draw water from the river or canal) or a plow, he shall pay three shekels in money.

261. If any one hire a herdsman for cattle or sheep, he shall pay him eight gur of corn per annum.

262. If any one, a cow or a sheep . . .

263. If he kill the cattle or sheep that were given to him, he shall compensate the owner with cattle for cattle and sheep for sheep.

264. If a herdsman, to whom cattle or sheep have been entrusted for watching over, and who has received his wages as agreed upon, and is satisfied, diminish the number of the cattle or sheep, or make the increase by birth less, he shall make good the increase or profit which was lost in the terms of settlement.

265. If a herdsman, to whose care cattle or sheep have been entrusted, be guilty of fraud and make false returns of the natural increase, or sell them for money, then shall he be convicted and pay the owner ten times the loss.

266. If the animal be killed in the stable by God (an accident), or if a lion kill it, the herdsman shall declare his innocence before God, and the owner bears the accident in the stable.

267. If the herdsman overlook something, and an accident happen in the stable, then the herdsman is at fault for the accident which he has caused in the stable, and he must compensate the owner for the cattle or sheep.

268. If any one hire an ox for threshing, the amount of the hire is twenty ka of corn.

269. If he hire an ass for threshing, the hire is twenty ka of corn.

270. If he hire a young animal for threshing, the hire is ten ka of corn.

271. If any one hire oxen, cart and driver, he shall pay one hundred and eighty ka of corn per day.

272. If any one hire a cart alone, he shall pay forty ka of corn per day.

273. If any one hire a day laborer, he shall pay him from the New Year until the fifth month (April to August, when days are long and the work hard) six gerahs in money per day; from the sixth month to the end of the year he shall give him five gerahs per day.

274. If any one hire a skilled artizan, he shall pay as wages of the . . . five gerahs, as wages of the potter five gerahs, of a tailor five gerahs, of . . . gerahs, . . . of a ropemaker four gerahs, of . . .. gerahs, of a mason . . . gerahs per day.

275. If any one hire a ferryboat, he shall pay three gerahs in money per day.

276. If he hire a freight-boat, he shall pay two and one-half gerahs per day.

277. If any one hire a ship of sixty gur, he shall pay one-sixth of a shekel in money as its hire per day.

278. If any one buy a male or female slave, and before a month has elapsed the benu-disease be developed, he shall return the slave to the seller, and receive the money which he had paid.

279. If any one buy a male or female slave, and a third party claim it, the seller is liable for the claim.

280. If while in a foreign country a man buy a male or female slave belonging to another of his own country; if when he return home the owner of the male or female slave recognize it: if the male or female slave be a native of the country, he shall give them back without any money.

281. If they are from another country, the buyer shall declare the amount of money paid therefor to the merchant, and keep the male or female slave.

282. If a slave say to his master: "You are not my master," if they convict him his master shall cut off his ear.

The Conclusion

A righteous law, and pious statute did he teach the land. Hammurabi, the protecting king am I. I have not withdrawn myself from the men, whom Bel gave to me, the rule over whom Marduk gave to me, I was not negligent, but I made them a peaceful abiding-place. I expounded all great difficulties, I made the light shine upon them. With the mighty weapons which Zamama and Ishtar entrusted to me, with the keen vision with which Ea endowed me, with the wisdom that Marduk gave me, I have uprooted the enemy above and below (in north and south), subdued the earth, brought prosperity to the land, guaranteed security to the inhabitants in their homes; a disturber was not permitted. The great gods have called me, I am the salvation-bearing shepherd, whose staff is straight, the good shadow that is spread over my city; on my breast I cherish the inhabitants of the land of Sumer and Akkad; in my shelter I have let them repose in peace; in my deep wisdom have I enclosed them. That the strong might not injure the weak, in order to protect the widows and orphans, I have in Babylon the city where Anu and Bel raise high their head, in E-Sagil, the Temple, whose foundations stand firm as heaven and earth, in order to bespeak justice in the land, to settle all disputes, and heal all injuries, set up these my precious words, written upon my memorial stone, before the image of me, as king of righteousness.

The king who ruleth among the kings of the cities am I. My words are well considered; there is no wisdom like unto mine. By the command of Shamash, the great judge of heaven and earth, let righteousness go forth in the land: by the order of Marduk, my lord, let no destruction befall my monument. In E-Sagil, which I love, let my name be ever repeated; let the oppressed, who has a case at law, come and stand before this my image as king of righteousness; let him read the inscription, and understand my precious words: the inscription will explain his case to him; he will find out what is just, and his heart will be glad, so that he will say:

"Hammurabi is a ruler, who is as a father to his subjects, who holds the words of Marduk in reverence, who has achieved conquest for Marduk over the north and south, who rejoices the heart of Marduk, his lord, who has bestowed benefits for ever and ever on his subjects, and has established order in the land."

When he reads the record, let him pray with full heart to Marduk, my lord, and Zarpanit, my lady; and then shall the protecting deities and the gods, who frequent E-Sagil, graciously grant the desires daily presented before Marduk, my lord, and Zarpanit, my lady.

In future time, through all coming generations, let the king, who may be in the land, observe the words of righteousness which I have written on my monument; let him not alter the law of the land which I have given, the edicts which I have enacted; my monument let him not mar. If such a ruler have wisdom, and be able to keep his land in order, he shall observe the words which I have written in this inscription; the rule, statute, and law of the land which I have given; the decisions which I have made will this inscription show him; let him rule his subjects accordingly, speak justice to them, give right decisions, root out the miscreants and criminals from this land, and grant prosperity to his subjects.

Hammurabi, the king of righteousness, on whom Shamash has conferred right (or law) am I. My words are well considered; my deeds are not equaled; to bring low those that were high; to humble the proud, to expel insolence. If a succeeding ruler considers my words, which I have written in this my inscription, if he do not annul my law, nor corrupt my words, nor change my monument, then may Shamash lengthen that king's reign, as he has that of me, the king of righteousness, that he may reign in righteousness over his subjects. If this ruler do not esteem my words, which I have written in my inscription, if he despise my curses, and fear not the curse of God, if he destroy the law which I have given, corrupt my words, change my monument, efface my name, write his name there, or on account of the curses commission another so to do, that man, whether king or ruler, patesi, or commoner, no matter what he be, may the great God (Anu), the Father of the gods, who has ordered my rule, withdraw from him the glory of royalty, break his scepter, curse his destiny. May Bel, the lord, who fixeth destiny, whose command can not be altered, who has made my kingdom great, order a rebellion which his hand can not control; may he let the wind of the overthrow of his habitation blow, may he ordain the years of his rule in groaning, years of scarcity, years of famine, darkness without light, death with seeing eyes be fated to him; may he (Bel) order with his potent mouth the destruction of his city, the dispersion of his subjects, the cutting off of his rule, the removal of his name and memory from the land. May Belit, the great Mother, whose command is potent in E-Kur (the Babylonian Olympus), the Mistress, who harkens graciously to my petitions, in the seat of judgment and decision (where Bel fixes destiny), turn his affairs evil before Bel, and put the devastation of his land, the destruction of his subjects, the pouring out of his life like water into the mouth of King Bel. May Ea, the great ruler, whose fated decrees come to pass, the thinker of the gods, the omniscient, who maketh long the days of my life, withdraw understanding and wisdom from him, lead him to forgetfulness, shut up his rivers at their sources, and not allow corn or sustenance for man to grow in his land. May Shamash, the great Judge of heaven and earth, who supporteth all means of livelihood, Lord of life-courage, shatter his dominion, annul his law, destroy his way, make vain the march of his troops, send him in his visions forecasts of the uprooting of the foundations of his throne and of the destruction of his land. May the condemnation of Shamash overtake him forthwith; may he be deprived of water above among the living, and his spirit below in the earth. May Sin (the Moon-god), the Lord of Heaven, the divine father, whose crescent gives light among the gods, take away the crown and regal throne from him; may he put upon him heavy guilt, great decay, that nothing may be lower than he. May he destine him as fated, days, months and years of dominion filled with sighing and tears, increase of the burden of dominion, a life that is like unto death. May Adad, the lord of fruitfulness, ruler of heaven and earth, my helper, withhold from him rain from heaven, and the flood of water from the springs, destroying his land by famine and want; may he rage mightily over his city, and make his land into flood-hills (heaps of ruined cities). May Zamama, the great warrior, the first-born son of E-Kur, who goeth at my right hand, shatter his weapons on the field of battle, turn day into night for him, and let his foe triumph over him. May Ishtar, the goddess of fighting and war, who unfetters my weapons, my gracious protecting spirit, who loveth my dominion, curse his kingdom in her angry heart; in her great wrath, change his grace into evil, and shatter his weapons on the place of fighting and war. May she create disorder and sedition for him, strike down his warriors, that the earth may drink their blood, and throw down the piles of corpses of his warriors on the field; may she not grant him a life of mercy, deliver him into the hands of his enemies, and imprison him in the land of his enemies. May Nergal, the might among the gods, whose contest is irresistible, who grants me victory, in his great might burn up his subjects like a slender reedstalk, cut off his limbs with his mighty weapons, and shatter him like an earthen image. May Nin-tu, the sublime mistress of the lands, the fruitful mother, deny him a son, vouchsafe him no name, give him no successor among men. May Nin-karak, the daughter of Anu, who adjudges grace to me, cause to come upon his members in E-kur high fever, severe wounds, that can not be healed, whose nature the physician does not understand, which he can not treat with dressing, which, like the bite of death, can not be removed, until they have sapped away his life.

May he lament the loss of his life-power, and may the great gods of heaven and earth, the Anunaki, altogether inflict a curse and evil upon the confines of the temple, the walls of this E-barra (the Sun temple of Sippara), upon his dominion, his land, his warriors, his subjects, and his troops. May Bel curse him with the potent curses of his mouth that can not be altered, and may they come upon him forthwith.